CLASSICAL *PIANO* SOLOS COLLECTION

VOLUME *EIGHT*

Wise Publications
London/New York/Paris/Sydney/Copenhagen/Madrid

Exclusive Distributors:

Music Sales Limited
8/9 Frith Street, London W1V 5TZ, England.

Music Sales Pty Limited
120 Rothschild Avenue, Rosebery, NSW 2018, Australia.

Music Sales Corporation
257 Park Avenue South, New York, NY10010, United States of America.

Order No. AM92420
ISBN 0-7119-4497-0

Book design by Studio Twenty, London
Computer management by Adam Hay Editorial Design
Compiled by Stephen Harding

Printed in the United Kingdom by
J.B. Offset Printers (Marks Tey) Limited, Marks Tey, Essex.

Allemande and Courante from Suite No.4

Composed by George Frideric Handel

Allegro moderato

Allegretto tranquillo
cresc.
dimin.
cresc.
calando
cresc.
cresc.
poco a poco decresc.
cresc.
calando

Bagatelle in G Minor
Op. 119, No. 1

Composed by Ludwig van Beethoven

cresc.
p
cresc.
f
p
dim.
pp

Ballade in G Minor
Op.118, No.3

Composed by Johannes Brahms

Ped.
dim.
dim. molto
p
pp una corda
col Ped.
espress.
dolce

pp
sempre p
dolce
rit.
dim.
poco sosten.
p
poco
a
cresc.
f
poco
a tempo
f
rit.
ten.
p
Ped.
Ped.
Ped.

Ped.
poco cresc.
cresc.
sf
f
ff
p
una corda
senza Ped.

Golliwog's Cake Walk
No.5 from Children's Corner

Composed by Claude Debussy

più p
Un peu moins vite
più p

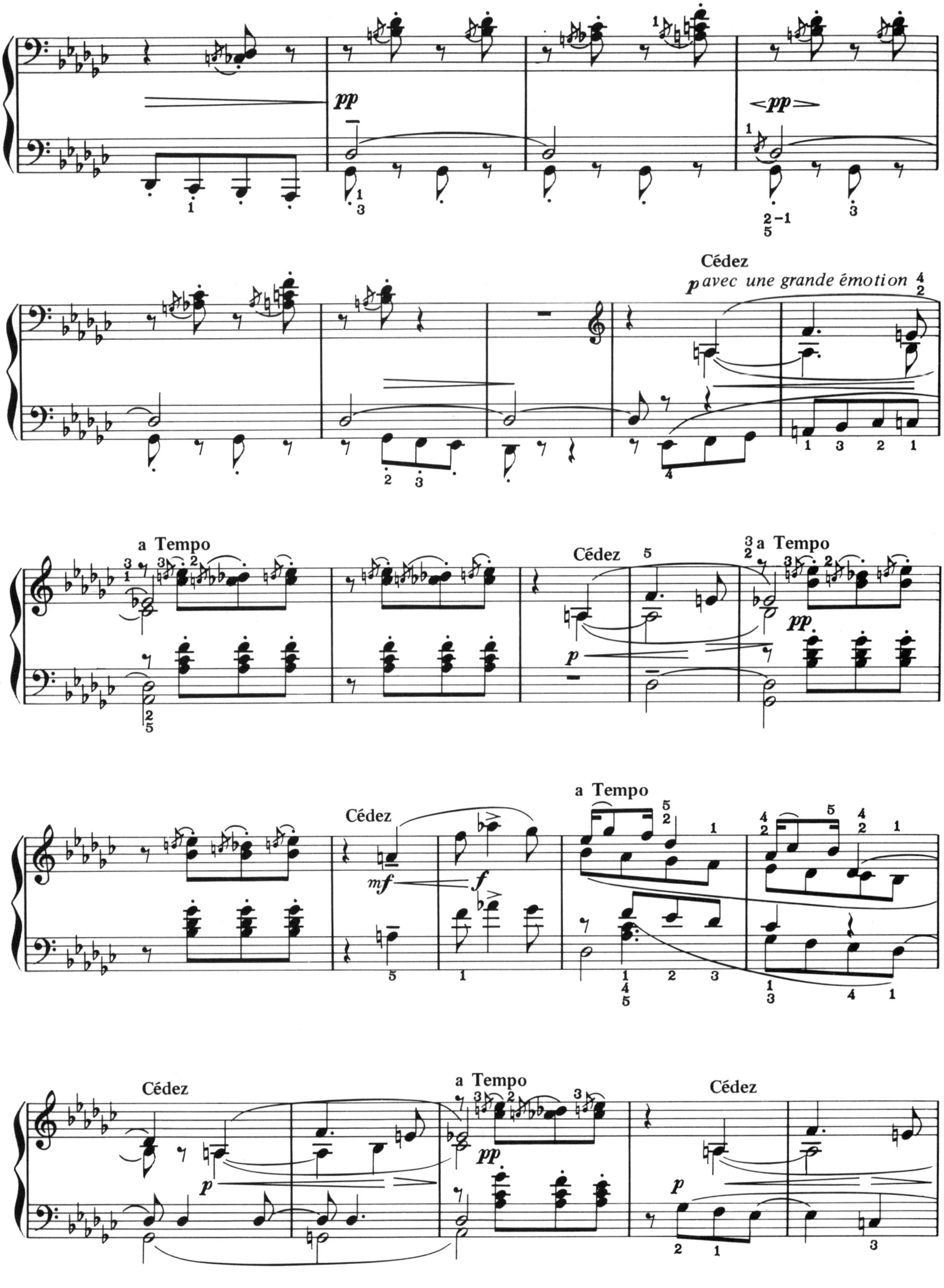
Cédez
p avec une grande émotion
a Tempo
Cédez
a Tempo
Cédez
a Tempo
Cédez
a Tempo
Cédez

a Tempo
dim.
Retenez
piu p
Toujours retenu
Tempo I°
molto

p cre - scen - do

Lyric Piece
Op.12, No.1 'Arietta'

Composed by Edvard Grieg

Impromptu in E♭ Major
Op.90/D.899, No.2

Composed by Franz Schubert

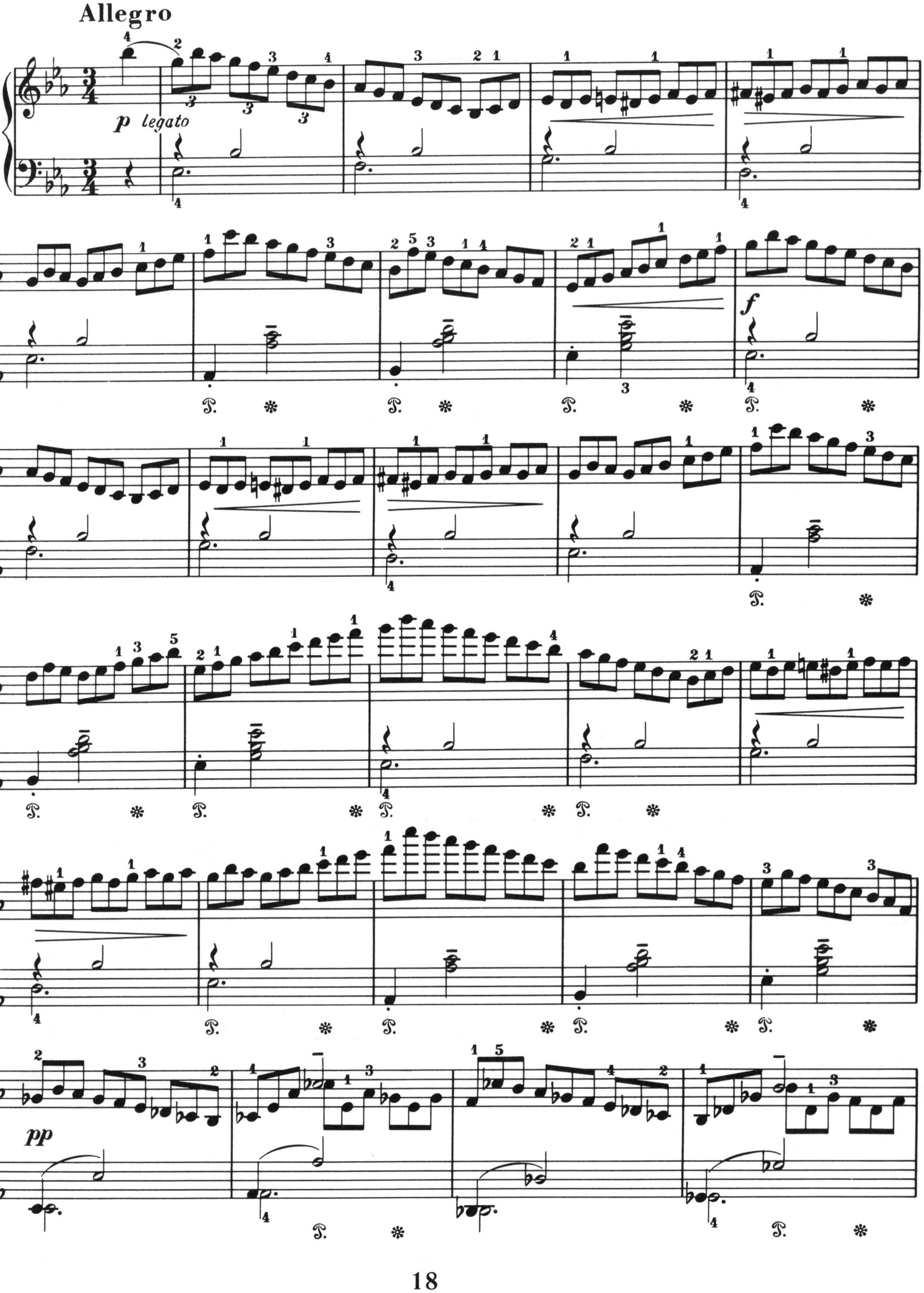

fp
fp
decresc.
p

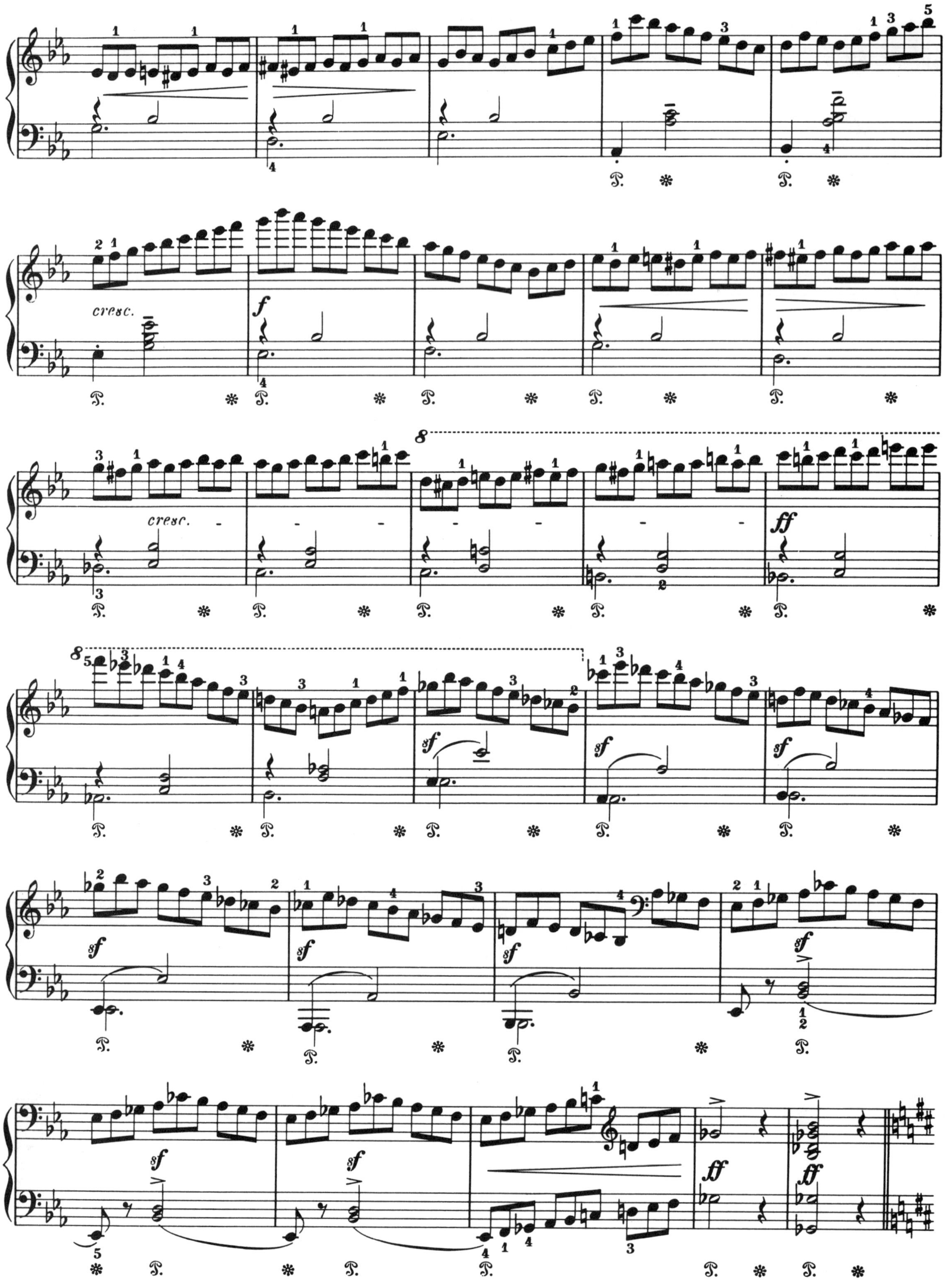

cresc.
cresc.

ben marcato

ff
fz
fz
p
f
p
f

cresc.
(mf)
decresc.

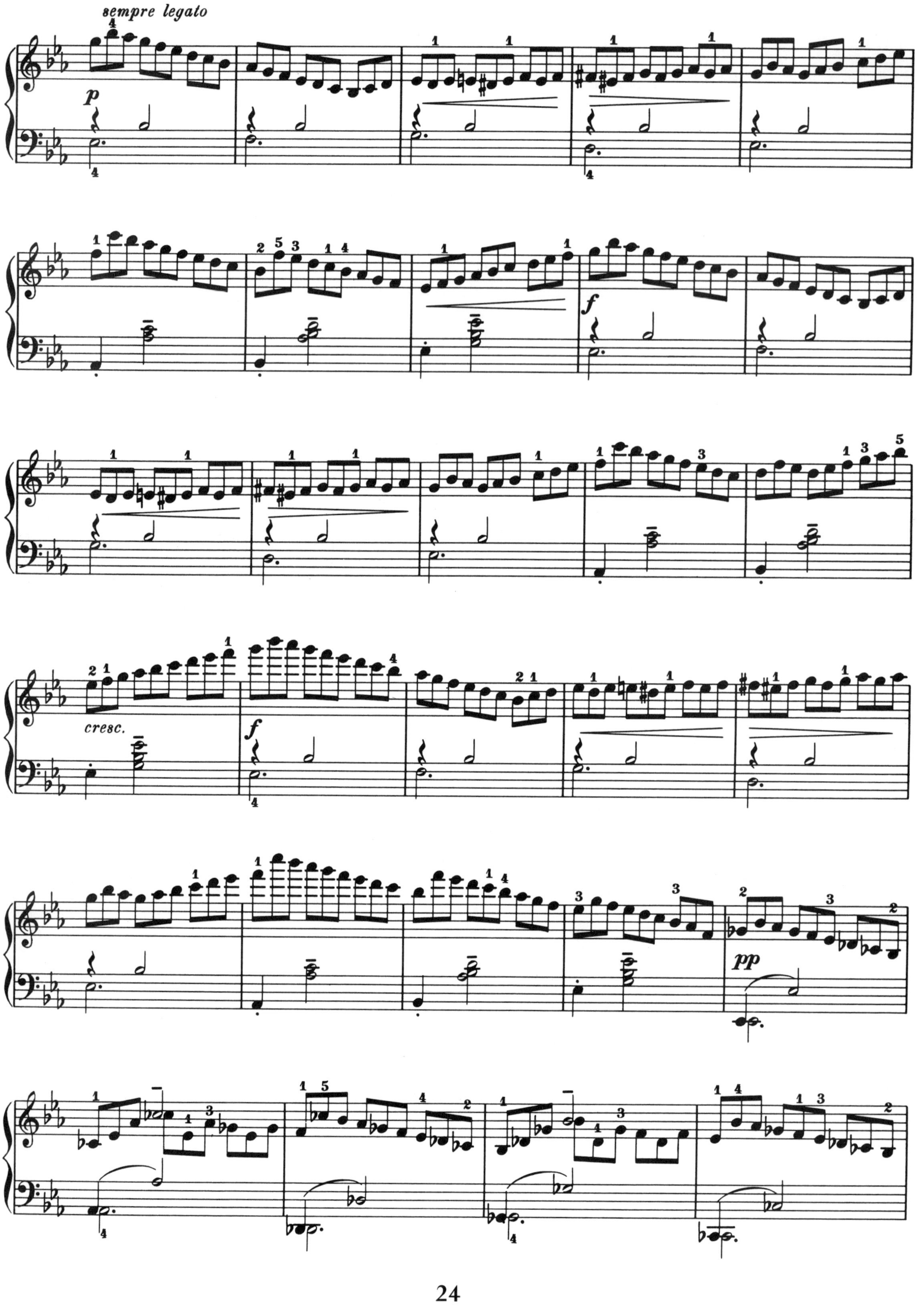
sempre legato
p
f
cresc.
f
pp

fp
fp
decresc.
p

cresc.
f
cresc.
ff
sf
ff

ff
ff
ff accelerando
fz

No.5 from Five Short Pieces

Composed by Lennox Berkeley

p
f
p
cresc.
f
ff

Pajaro Triste
from Impresiones Intimas

Composed by Federico Mompou

p
sfz
rit
accel.
cresc.
cen
do
p
a tempo
pp
sfz
rit
a tempo
p
espress.
pp
p
rit.
dolce
pp

Piano Sonata in C Major
Hob XVI:35 - 1st Movement

Composed by Joseph Haydn

cresc.
cresc.

fz
fz
fz
fz
fz
p
cresc.
f
cresc.
ff
decresc.
Adagio Tempo I
p
p
fz

f
fz
fz
p
mf
f
ff
p
cresc.
p
pp
f
p
f

Piano Sonata No.14 in C# Minor
Op.27, No.2 'Moonlight' - 1st Movement

Composed by Ludwig van Beethoven

una corda
marcato, ma sempre p
pp
cresc.
dimin.
p una corda
pp
il basso sempre
p
pp

pp
p
cresc.
dim.
espress.
p
mf
dim.
una corda
più marcato del principio
poco riten.
a tempo
pp
grave
p
p
un poco
Ped.
cresc.
più cresc.
p subito
Ped.

piu p
pp
Ped
sempre legatissimo
una corda
dimin.
slentando
pp
ppp

Sinfonia (3-Part Invention) No.4
BWV790

Composed by Johann Sebastian Bach

Song Without Words in C Major
Op.102, No.3

Composed by Felix Mendelssohn-Bartholdy

(poco cresc.)
p
sempre staccato al fine
sf
dimin.
p
(cresc.)
sf
(dimin.)
p
dimin.
pp (leggierissimo)

Prelude in D♭ Major
Op.25, No.5 'Raindrop'

Composed by Frédéric Chopin

sotto voce
cresc.
p cresc.
ff
dimin.
p
cresc.
p cresc.
ff

fz dimin.
cresc.
dim. e rit.
10
smorzando
e slentando
riten.